THE GREAT LEOPARD HUNT

WRITTEN & ILLUSTRATED
by **CAROLYN MACY**

The Great Leopard Hunt - Coloring Book
Copyright © 2017 by Carolyn Macy. All rights reserved.

No part of this publication may be reproduced, stored in a retrieval system or transmitted in any way by any means, electronic, mechanical, photocopy, recording or otherwise without the prior permission of the author except as provided by USA copyright law.

Published by Carolyn Macy
6227 81st Avenue N.E. | Norman, Oklahoma 73026 USA
405.401.2012

Book design copyright © 2017 by Carolyn Macy.
Written and Illustrated by Carolyn Macy

Published in the United States of America
ISBN: 978-0-9989127-8-3
1. JUVENILE NONFICTION / Animals / Jungle Animals
2. JUVENILE NONFICTION / History / United States / Oklahoma

The jungle loomed dark and the jungle lay deep
With secrets it guarded and promised to keep,
From its canopied top to its deepest ravine,
By hiding its life in dense foliage of green.

Spied resting atop of a branch on a tree,
And drowsily watching all things he could see,
Lay a leopard in prime in his fine, spotted coat
With rumbling contentment escaping his throat.

The Fates had decreed that this leopard who lay,
Stretched out and enjoying the warmth of the day
In his India jungle, would journey abroad
To plains far away where the Indians trod.

One warm winter day as some winter days go,
This fine captured feline kept pacing below
While his eyes searched above for a place he could leap
To escape from this prison so rocky and deep.

His amber eyes narrowed ablaze with their glow.
Fierce anger welled up, and his throat rumbled low.
With a flick of his tail and brute muscle control,
His body released and took flight with his soul.

Some boys, who stood watching above by the fence,
Fell back in surprised and in speechless suspense
When his claws gripped the rail where he came to a stop,
And blazing, wild eyes met their eyes at the top.

Brief moments he balanced on top of the rail,
Just looking around to determine his trail.
Past memories rose to help show him the way
And beckoned him towards them this warm,
winter day.

To get back in his jungle
 to roam wild and free
Filled much of his mind,
 just as much as could be.

So straightway he leaped
 to flee fast from the zoo,
And frightened some folks
 when he came in their view.

He raced for his freedom with all of his might.
He raced toward the woods that he held in his sight.
That tawny, fine form disappeared in those trees.
Zookeepers seemed shocked he escaped with such ease.

Vast rumors ran rampant as where he had strayed.
This wild, spotted feline had people afraid.
The "Great Hunt" began for this wild, escaped beast.
Each moment the reign of his terror increased.

Folks peeked around corners,
in bushes, and under.
All shadows could move, and
each noise made them wonder.

The whole countryside
    became jumpy and scared
For he had not been found,
    and he had not been snared.

Marines and the Red Cross
each mobilized too.
They combed all the places
surrounding the zoo.

"Lion dogs" led the hunt,
  and folks trailed with their pets
To help track the feline
  that caused all the threats.

By air, helicopters and planes
joined the search.
For three days they scanned
from their lofty sky perch.

Civil Air and police rallied...
 even the press
Got in on the hunt,
 but with little success.

His tracks in some mud
   by a pond folks discovered;
A farm where some cattle
   stampeded they covered.

One section of brush grown
 so thick needed burned,
But the leopard's location
 remained to be learned.

Some meat that was soaked in a sleep remedy
Was placed by his cage for the leopard to see.
When his hunger once brought his return to the zoo,
They'd be ready and poised for the cat rendezvous.

Under cover of darkness when hunger grew great,
The leopard returned for the meat, which he ate.
So groggy he grew that he hardly could creep
Where they found him curled up in his tunnel asleep.

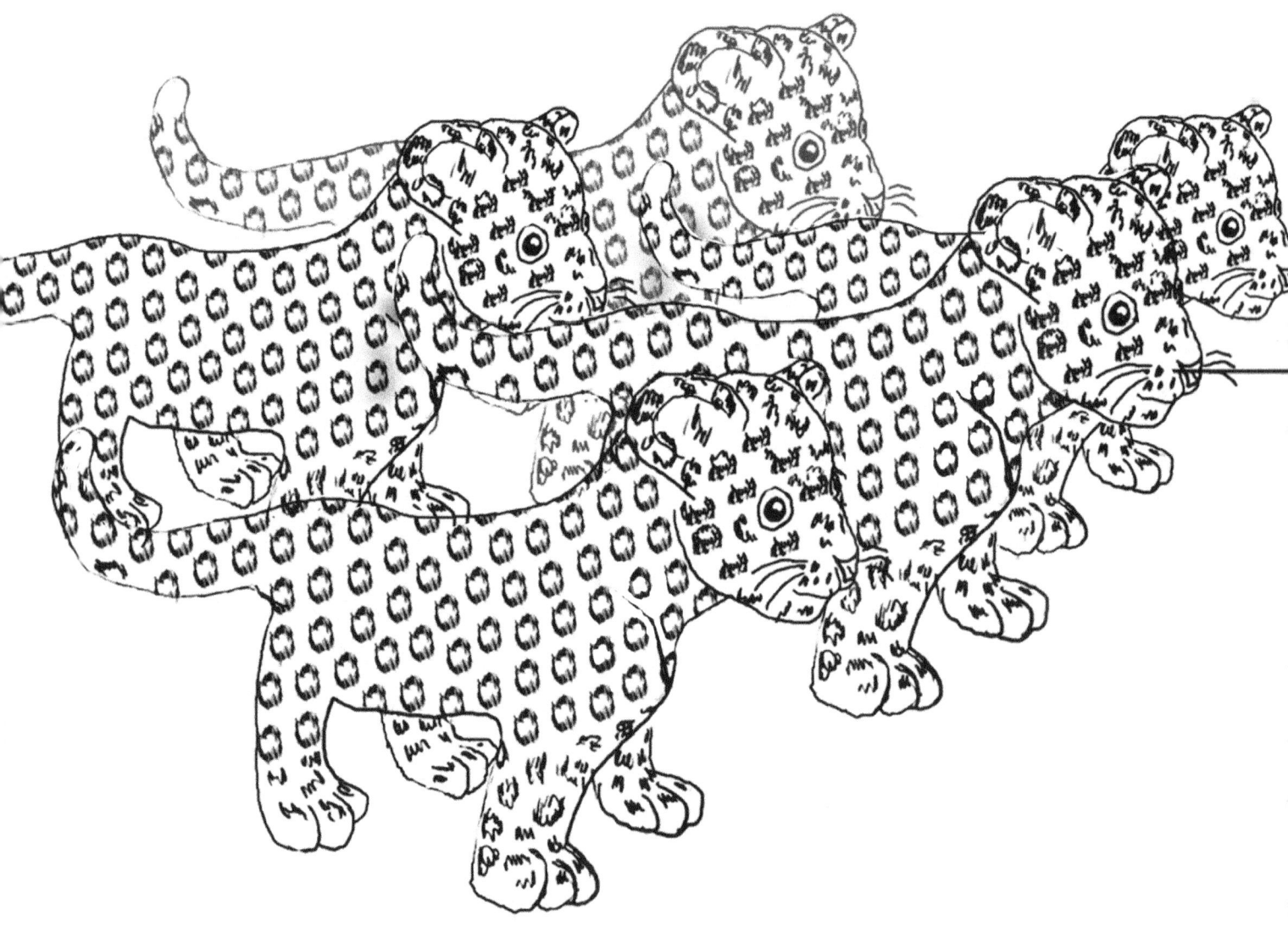

Once he returned, the press
gave him a name,
Known simply as "Leapy",
to honor his fame.

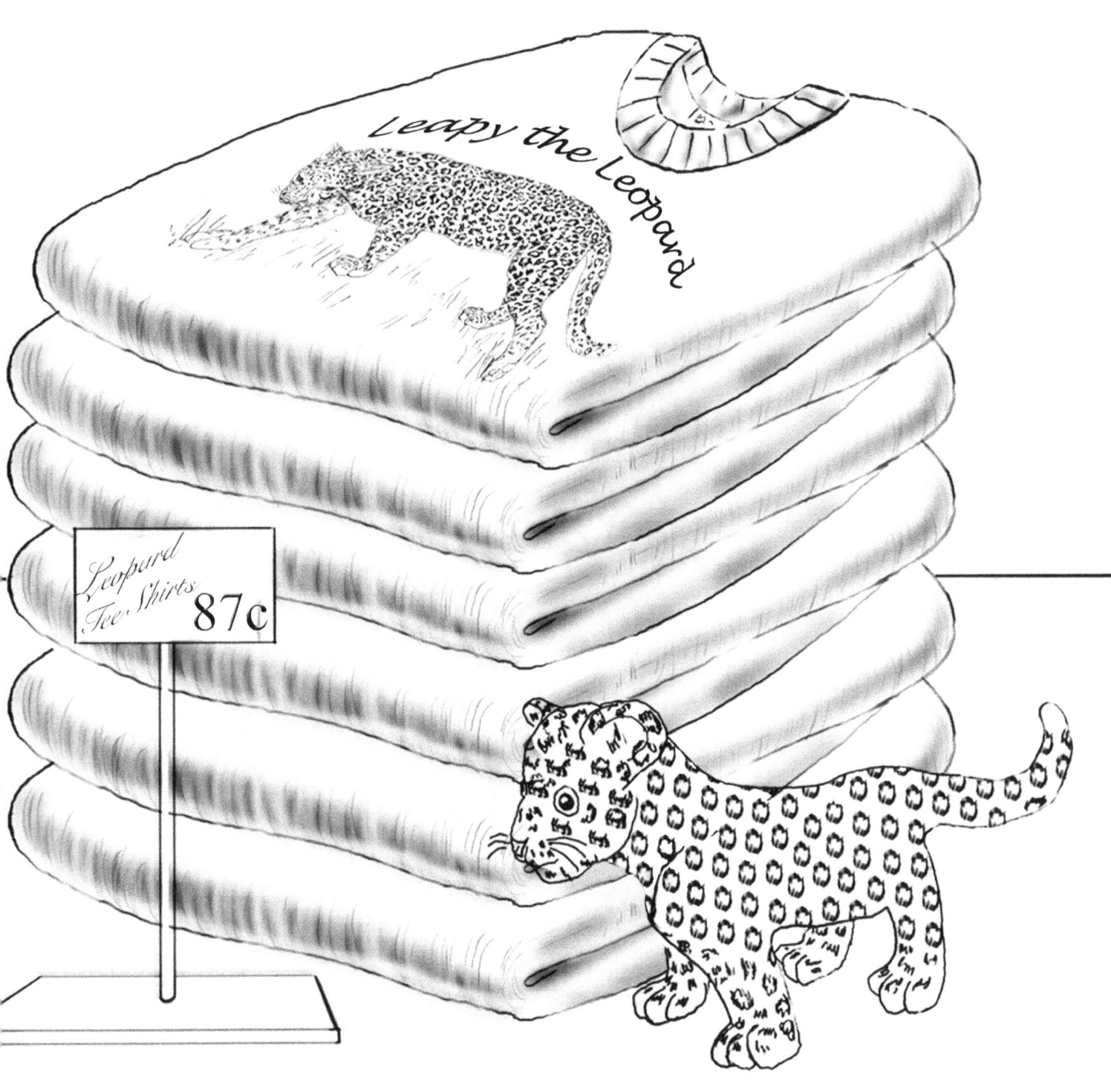

With the "Great Hunt" now over
with all of its noise,
Store merchants sold t-shirts
and stuffed leopard toys!

Zookeepers made "Leapy" a room with a view
After once he returned to the OKC Zoo.
There from his new quarters, folks watched him with ease,
And through its glass wall, he could still see his trees.